A millennium celebration

TEN RELIGIOUS MASTERPIECES FROM THE ROYAL COLLECTION

A millennium celebration

Jane Roberts

THE ROYAL COLLECTION

First published 2000 by Royal Collection Enterprises Limited,
St James's Palace, London SW1A 1JR
http://www.royal.gov.uk

ISBN 1 902163 75 3
A catalogue record for this book is available from the British Library

Typeset in Centaur
Designed by Sally McIntosh
Produced by Book Production Consultants plc,
25–27 High Street, Chesterton, Cambridge CB4 1ND
Printed and bound in Great Britain by The Wolsey Press, Ipswich
Distributed by Thames and Hudson Ltd,
181A High Holborn, London WC1V 7QX

This publication accompanies the Royal Collection travelling exhibition
which will be shown at the following locations in 2000:
Ulster Museum, Belfast (28 JANUARY–26 MARCH)
Southampton City Art Gallery (7 APRIL–4 JUNE)
The Hunterian Art Gallery, University of Glasgow (16 JUNE–16 SEPTEMBER)
Laing Art Gallery, Newcastle upon Tyne (14 OCTOBER–10 DECEMBER)
The exhibition will then be shown for a limited period at The Gallery, Windsor Castle.

Author's Acknowledgements
The assistance of my father-in-law, The Rt Revd Dr Edward Roberts, and of my colleague,
Martin Clayton, in the preparation of this publication is gratefully acknowledged.

All works reproduced are in the Royal Collection unless otherwise indicated.
Permission for other reproductions has been granted by the following:
Florence, Ente Casa Buonarroti, fig. 12; Florence, Fratelli Alinari, figs 8, 10, 12; Florence, Galleria degli Uffizi, figs 8, 10;
London, British Museum, fig. 7; Madrid, Museo del Prado, fig. 9; Milan, Museo d'Arte Antica del Castello Sforzesco, fig. 13;
Milan, Soprintendenza, fig. 11; Paris, Musée du Louvre: © Photo RMN, figs 1, 3, 5; Prague, Národni Muzeum, fig. 2.

Front cover GIOVANNI FRANCESCO BARBIERI (*called* GUERCINO), *The Annunciation* (no. 2, enlarged detail)
Frontispiece MICHELANGELO BUONARROTI, *The Risen Christ* (no. 10, enlarged detail)

Contents

ST. JAMES'S PALACE

This exhibition is subtitled 'a millennium celebration'. Amidst all the noise and confusion which has characterised our commemoration of the two thousandth anniversary of the birth of Christ, I can think of few more fitting ways of marking this extraordinary moment in history than by quietly contemplating these marvellous images.

Ten Religious Masterpieces brings together depictions of aspects of the life of Christ by artists universally acknowledged to be amongst the greatest of the second millennium. Leonardo da Vinci and Michelangelo are generously represented. They were active in the middle years of this millennium at a time of huge changes in the ways in which our forebears thought, not least about Christ. Jane Roberts describes their era in her introduction, touching on some of the reasons for the extraordinary impact of this art on us today.

These are some of the gems in the Royal Collection and I am proud of, and hugely grateful for, the discrimination shown by Charles II and George III in acquiring them. The drawings have been on public display before, of course, but The Queen and the Trustees of the Royal Collection are determined that they should be as widely seen as possible. This exhibition will take them to a new public beyond the capital, and I do hope that all those who visit it will derive as much joy from the pictures as I have always done.

Introduction

The works included in this exhibition have been selected in order to represent the story of the Life of Christ as drawn by some of the greatest masters in the history of Western art. The sequence approximately follows that recounted in the Bible (summarised on pages 17–20).

Traditionally, the function of art – whether religious or secular – is to delight the eye and mind, and to inform. The latter purpose was particularly relevant at a time when the biblical narrative could not be read by more than a small proportion of the population. A further fundamental purpose of religious art is to provide images that will be the object of private devotion.

The main events described in the New Testament have been treated by artists since early in the first millennium. There are depictions of Christ's Baptism, Crucifixion and Resurrection from the fourth and fifth centuries. Later, the Virgin Mary came to dominate devotional imagery. With the foundation of the Franciscan and Dominican Orders in the early thirteenth century, the use of visual images to accompany and stimulate prayer and worship was encouraged. While preachers taught their congregations to consider the humanity of Christ and the Virgin, artists began to represent the sacred characters as recognisable people, in the style

and dress of their own time. They also showed the Virgin and Child with a close physical relationship, such as that enjoyed by a contemporary mother and child (see nos 6 and 7). As a result of the technical advances made in the Renaissance period, artists were also able to convey the movement and reactions of figures in a convincing manner. The *Risen Christ* drawn by Michelangelo thus serves as an ideal of classical and eternal beauty (no. 10).

The works in this catalogue span the period between the late fifteenth and the mid-seventeenth centuries, the years of the Renaissance and Reformation, and of the Counter-Reformation and its immediate aftermath. The earliest of the exhibited drawings (nos 3, 6) were made by Leonardo da Vinci in Florence in the 1470s. There are single drawings, also by Leonardo, produced in Milan in the 1490s (no. 8) and in Milan or Rome two decades later (no. 1). Leonardo was the epitome of the 'universal man' described in the Humanist literature of the Italian Renaissance. Although he wrote (in the *Treatise on Painting*) that 'The good painter has two principal things to paint: that is, man and the intention of his mind', it was clearly understood that the chief vehicle of this idealism was religious art. It is no accident that Leonardo's best-known works are the *Virgin of the Rocks* (fig. 1) and the *Last Supper* (fig. 11).

Fig. 1 LEONARDO DA VINCI
*The Virgin of the Rocks, c.*1483–6
(Paris, Musée du Louvre)

All but one of the drawings are by Italian draughtsmen. The exception is no. 5, by the German artist Albrecht Dürer. His drawing is dated 1519, the year of Leonardo's death. This was also the year in which Dürer was described (by a fellow artist, Jan van Scorel) as being fully occupied with the 'teachings by which Luther had begun to stir the quiet world'. Martin Luther, the German friar whose *Ninety-five Theses* (published in 1517) mark the start of the Reformation proper, was critical of the teaching and conduct of the Church of Rome and in particular of the sale of indulgences. Indulgences were remissions of the punishment due for past sins; they were granted following the performance of good or worthy acts, such as the gift of money (or even works of art) to a church. The conduct of the head of the Church, the Pope, was also called into question by Luther and his fellow reformers. In 1514 the northern Humanist Desiderius Erasmus had published a satire against Pope Julius II which described St Peter refusing entry to the Pope ('a sink of iniquity') at the gates of Heaven.

Julius II, who had died in the previous year, is chiefly known to art historians as the enlightened patron of Bramante, Raphael and Michelangelo. The exhibition contains three works by Michelangelo, who was born in 1475, four years after Dürer and twenty-three years after Leonardo. In the course of his long life, Michelangelo became closely involved with those in Rome who were seeking to reform the Church from within. There is a profound sense of spirituality in all of Michelangelo's religious art, whether his early sculpture (fig. 12), the paintings on the Sistine ceiling, the designs of the 1530s (nos 7 and 10), the *Last Judgement* fresco, or the intense and highly individual works produced towards the end of his long life (including no. 9 and figs 7, 13).

Michelangelo lived through the religious and political crisis of 1527, when the troops of the Holy Roman Emperor Charles V descended through Italy to Rome, the seat of the papacy. While Luther and others had been calling for Church reform for many years, the 'Sack of Rome' forced the Roman Catholic Church itself to recognise the need for action. A Church Council was now summoned to establish and restate the central articles of belief and liturgy of the Church; it met in Trent (a small town on the Adige in northern Italy) for three sessions between 1545 and 1563. As a result of the Council the sale of indulgences was forbidden, the role of the sacraments and the power of the papacy were reaffirmed, and the training and conduct of the clergy became the subject of numerous rules and regulations. Inevitably the Council's deliberations had a profound effect on religious art, which was now particularly promoted as a useful support to religious teaching. Depictions of religious themes were to be clear, simple and intelligible; they were to be interpreted realistically; and they were to include an emotional stimulus to piety. In addition,

Fig. 2   ALBRECHT DÜRER
The Feast of the Rosegarlands, 1506
(Prague, Národni Muzeum)

religious works of art were now to be scrutinised by the clergy to ensure that they were both accurate and fitting. The naked forms which are such a notable feature of Michelangelo's Passion subjects (including nos 9 and 10) were no longer considered suitable and in 1564 orders were issued for the covering of the 'obscene parts' of the figures in the *Last Judgement*.

The implementation of these new rules and regulations, together with the use of coercion (the Inquisition or Holy Office), were the chief features of the Counter-Reformation

movement of the later sixteenth century. In spite of the efforts of churchmen to ensure that religious art served their cause, much painting and sculpture of this period is characterised by obscure iconography, exaggerated gestures and stylised figures, hence the term 'Mannerism' which has been used to describe it. However, in the early seventeenth century painted religious imagery became more direct and thus of more use to the Church. In Guercino's drawing of

(*above*) Fig. 3 RAPHAEL
The Virgin and Child with the Infant
St John the Baptist (La Belle Jardinière), 1507
(Paris, Musée du Louvre)

(*right*) Fig. 4 ALBRECHT DÜRER
The Virgin and Child, c.1518
(engraving; BARTSCH 39; RCIN 800052)

(*opposite*) Fig. 5 LEONARDO DA VINCI
The Virgin and Child and St Anne, c.1510–17
(Paris, Musée du Louvre)

the *Annunciation* (no. 2), datable *c*.1618, little detracts from the central moment in this religious drama, in which the youth and purity of the Virgin Mary are implicit. The work of Castiglione demonstrates a rather different facet of seventeenth-century art; in spite of the potentially restrictive nature of the Counter-Reformation instructions concerning religious imagery, there was still scope for inventive approaches. From *c*.1630 Castiglione transformed a number of well-tried themes, without arousing the Church's hostility (see no. 4 and fig. 6).

A large proportion of all art produced in Europe between the fifteenth and seventeenth centuries was religious. Christianity was an intrinsic part of life at the time, for the Church ran the schools, the hospitals and other charitable activities as well as administering the sacraments and preaching. Even an artist such as Leonardo da Vinci, who was not noted for his personal spirituality, depended on the Church for much of his work. Leonardo's anatomical research was carried out in the monasteries of Florence, Milan and Rome, which provided the medical care for the local population. Occasionally (as with Fra Angelico and Fra Bartolommeo) a member of a religious order acquired the status of a professional artist. Much religious patronage was connected with the desire of an individual to reduce the

time spent in Purgatory after death and to obtain eternal salvation. This was particularly the case if the patron was involved in an activity such as usury (money-lending), which was deemed to be one of the Seven Deadly Sins.

The external and internal walls of buildings were thus covered with painted narratives of the sacred stories, while churches and chapels received new altarpieces (figs 1–3) and devotional pieces (e.g. fig. 9) were ordered for private homes. As the practice of forming

(*below*) Fig. 6
Giovanni Benedetto Castiglione
*The Virgin and Child with God the Father, c.*1650
(etching; Bartsch 7; RCIN 830452)

collections of works of art evolved, patrons vied with one another to obtain paintings and sculptures – whether sacred or secular – by the best artists, both to adorn their dwellings and to enrich their intellectual and spiritual lives.

The drawings in this exhibition were produced as part of this process. One was made in preparation for a mural painting (no. 8 and fig. 11). Another is connected with a panel painting (no. 1 and fig. 5). Three drawings (nos 2, 3 and 6) may also have been made in preparation for specific projects but it is not known whether they were ever used. Three of the remaining drawings (nos 4, 9 and 10) – and possibly nos 5 and 7 too – appear to have

been made as independent works of art. As such they are on one level more limited than paintings, for they lack the extra dimension of colour. But drawings preserve – and communicate to us – more of the artist's original intention than many a battered mural or discoloured panel painting. This is particularly apparent when we compare a monument of Western art such as Leonardo's mural of the *Last Supper* (fig. 11) with the studies that were made in preparation for the painting. The mural itself has suffered severe deterioration from damp penetration and misguided restoration in the past, leading to numerous irreversible paint losses. However, by

looking at Leonardo's drawing of Judas (no. 8), for example, we can imagine how the figure may once have appeared. This drawing, and the others at Windsor Castle relating to the mural, were frequently referred to by Dottoressa Pinin Brambilla Barcilon in the course of her recent conservation work on the *Last Supper*.

Before turning to those drawings which were created as independent works of art, we may be struck by the inherent unsuitability of a small and vulnerable sheet of paper for a devotional purpose – a purpose that was usually filled by a sturdy panel, a mural painting or even a piece of sculpture. But the fifteenth-century flowering of the engraving and woodcut as independent art forms provides a clear indication that small-scale works of art on paper were popular at the time. The fact that many of these early prints had religious subjects, and that a number have the appearance of devotional images (e.g. figs 4 and 14), demonstrates the wide currency of such 'paper imagery'. The graphic work of Castiglione shows that there was still a market for religious prints in the mid-seventeenth century (fig. 6).

A rare documented case of the way in which religious drawings were used and treasured in the Italian Renaissance occurs in the correspondence between Michelangelo and the noble poetess Vittoria Colonna, to whom the artist sent at least three drawings with

Fig. 7
MICHELANGELO BUONARROTI
Christ on the Cross, c.1540
(London, British Museum)

subjects relating to Christ's Passion. In a letter of *c.*1540 Vittoria acknowledged her receipt of a drawing showing Christ on the Cross (fig. 7) and commented: 'It is not possible to see an image better made, more alive and more finished and certainly I could never explain how subtly and marvellously wrought it is ... I have looked at it carefully in the light, with the glass, and with the mirror and I have never seen a more finished thing.' In another letter Vittoria expresses her delight that the angel on Christ's right is more beautiful than that on his left, for on the Last Day St Michael will place Michelangelo himself on Christ's right hand. She will address her prayers to *questo dolce Christo*, this sweet Christ.

When an artist drew or painted a religious subject he would make use of a number of different written sources, the most important of which was the Bible. Reliance on the Scriptures is an enduring feature of Christianity, but there was no mention in the Bible of some of the most popular subjects treated by artists in the fifteenth and sixteenth centuries. Narrative accounts of the life of the Virgin and of the early saints were instead found in apocryphal and legendary texts. The writings and sermons delivered by the popular preachers of the fourteenth and fifteenth centuries provided additional glosses and insights into biblical subjects. Thus the *Meditations on the Life of Christ* by a writer known as the Pseudo-Bonaventura (1300) described how the first meeting of the Christ Child and John the Baptist (see nos 6 and 7) took place when the Holy Family stayed with the Virgin's cousin, Elisabeth, on their return from Egypt. At the same time, mystery plays enacted holy stories for popular enlightenment and entertainment. The symbolism of the cross held by the young Baptist (see no. 7), of flowers such as the lily (see nos 2 and 3), and of fruit such as the apple (see no. 5), was elaborated upon in these contexts. Whether contemporary artists were acquainted with these particular texts is not strictly relevant. However, it is important for us to be aware of them in order to understand the ideas that were circulating in Renaissance Europe. The Reformation movement sought to wipe out the proliferation of non-biblical sources and thus reduced the number of sacred themes that were deemed suitable for treatment by artists. Art and artists suffered in consequence, although the drawings by Guercino and Castiglione shown here demonstrate that by the early seventeenth century works of sublime beauty on key religious themes were once again being produced.

The Life of Christ
as recorded in the New Testament

The incarnate Life of Jesus Christ is narrated in the four Gospels in the New Testament, quoted here in the Authorised King James Version (1611).

The Annunciation

The forthcoming birth of the Saviour, Jesus Christ, was announced to his mother, Mary, by the Angel Gabriel. 'And the angel came in unto her, and said, Hail, thou that art highly favoured, the Lord is with thee: blessed art thou among women. And when she saw him, she was troubled at his saying, and cast in her mind what manner of salutation this should be. And the angel said unto her, Fear not, Mary: for thou hast found favour with God. And, behold, thou shalt conceive in thy womb, and bring forth a son, and shalt call his name Jesus' (Luke 1: 28–31).

The Nativity and Childhood of Jesus

Shortly before the birth of Christ, Mary and Joseph travelled to Bethlehem, in the province of Judaea, so that they could be registered in a population census organised by the Roman administrators. Jesus was thus born away from home, in a stable, because 'there was no room for them in the inn' (Luke 2: 7). Little is recorded of his childhood, but at the age of 12 he is described discoursing with the scribes in the Temple.

Fig. 8 LEONARDO DA VINCI
The Annunciation, c.1473
(Florence, Galleria degli Uffizi;
photo Alinari)

Fig. 9 RAPHAEL
The Holy Family with the Lamb, 1507
(Madrid, Museo del Prado)

St John the Baptist

John, the forerunner and herald of Christ, was the son of the priest Zacharias and his wife Elisabeth and was born when both his parents were 'well stricken in years' (Luke 1: 7). The Virgin Mary was Elisabeth's kinswoman; the Annunciation of Christ's birth to the Virgin took place in the sixth month of Elisabeth's pregnancy.

The adult John was an itinerant preacher in the region around the River Jordan. 'John did baptize in the wilderness, and preach the baptism of repentance for the remission of sins' (Mark 1: 4). 'And it came to pass in those days, that Jesus came from Nazareth of Galilee, and was baptized of John in Jordan. And straightway coming up out of the water, he saw the heavens opened, and the Spirit like a dove descending upon him: and there came a voice from heaven, saying, Thou art my beloved Son, in whom I am well pleased' (Mark 1: 9–11).

The Temptation and Ministry of Jesus Christ

The baptism of Jesus was preceded by forty days in the wilderness, when numerous temptations were offered by the devil. Jesus now 'came into Galilee, preaching the gospel of the kingdom of God, and saying, The time is fulfilled, and the kingdom of God is at hand: repent ye, and believe the gospel' (Mark 1: 14–15). He gathered together a number of disciples, including the fishermen Simon (later surnamed Peter by Jesus), Andrew and the brothers James and John. The twelve specially chosen disciples

or apostles were instructed to go forth and preach 'as sheep in the midst of wolves' (Matthew 10: 16).

The success of Jesus' ministry aroused the suspicion and enmity of the Pharisees, a group among the Jews that was noted for strict observance of the law and of religious ordinances. Jesus retired with his disciples to the Gentile territories of Tyre and Sidon and – in the Transfiguration – revealed himself to his followers as the promised Messiah, hinting at his coming Passion, death and Resurrection.

(*left*) Fig. 10 ANDREA DEL VERROCCHIO with the assistance of LEONARDO DA VINCI
The Baptism of Christ, c.1470
(Florence, Galleria degli Uffizi; photo Alinari)

(*top, left*) Fig. 11 LEONARDO DA VINCI
The Last Supper, c.1495–7
(Milan, S. Maria delle Grazie)

(*top, right*) Fig. 12 MICHELANGELO BUONARROTI
The Santo Spirito Crucifix, ?1492
(Florence, Casa Buonarroti, in deposit from Santo Spirito; photo Alinari)

The Last Supper, Passion and Crucifixion

One week before the feast of the Jewish Passover, Jesus returned to Jerusalem with a large gathering of supporters. At the final meal which he shared with his disciples (the Last Supper), bread and wine were blessed and shared among those present. At the supper table Jesus announced that one of those present would betray him. His prophecy came to pass that evening, in the Garden of Gethsemane, when Judas led a group from the Temple towards Jesus and his fellow disciples, and identified his master by kissing his cheek. Jesus was arrested, tried and sentenced to death.

The mob, incited to hatred by the Pharisees, mocked and tormented Jesus on his way to Calvary, the place chosen for his Crucifixion. They placed a crown of thorns on his head and fixed him to a cross between two thieves. 'Now there stood by the cross of Jesus his mother, and his mother's sister, Mary the wife of Cleophas, and Mary Magdalene. When Jesus therefore saw his mother, and the

Fig. 13 MICHELANGELO BUONARROTI
The Rondanini Pietà, c.1552–64
(Milan, Museo d'Arte Antica
del Castello Sforzesco)

disciple standing by, whom he loved, he saith unto his mother, Woman, behold thy son! Then saith he to the disciple, Behold thy mother!' (John 19: 25–7). After six hours on the cross, 'Jesus cried with a loud voice, and gave up the ghost. And the veil of the temple was rent in twain from the top to the bottom' (Mark 15: 37–8). Joseph of Arimathaea was then given permission to take down the body. He 'laid him in a sepulchre which was hewn out of a rock, and rolled a stone unto the door of the sepulchre' (Mark 15: 46).

The Resurrection, Ascension and Pentecost

On the third day following the Crucifixion (Easter Day), the sepulchre was found to be open, and Jesus' body was no longer within. In the period leading to his Ascension, Christ appeared to a number of people, including his disciples at Emmaus. After forty days Christ went with his apostles to the Mount of Olives, where 'he was taken up; and a cloud received him out of their sight' (Acts 1: 9). The apostles then returned to Jerusalem. On the day of the Jewish feast of Pentecost, 'suddenly there came a sound from heaven as of a rushing mighty wind ... and they were all filled with the Holy Ghost' (Acts 2: 2–4).

Fig. 14 ALBRECHT DÜRER
The Resurrection, 1510
(woodcut; BARTSCH 15; RCIN 800128)

The Catalogue

I   LEONARDO DA VINCI (1452–1519)
The Head of St Anne

St Anne is traditionally identified as the mother of the Virgin Mary. This beautiful drawing was used for the head of St Anne in Leonardo's painting of the *Virgin and Child and St Anne* (Paris, Louvre; fig. 5). In that picture the Virgin sits on her mother's lap and leans out towards the Christ Child, who plays with a lamb at right. In the drawing, as in the painting, the eyes of St Anne are lowered towards the Christ Child. The lamb was used to symbolise sacrifice in ancient religions, and for Christians it represents Christ in his sacrificial role.

Although there is no mention of the Virgin's parents in the Bible, a second-century text (*The Protevangelium of James*) gives an apocryphal account of Mary's birth to Joachim and Anne. This narrative, retold in the *Golden Legend* in the thirteenth century, was the basis for countless representations of the life of the Virgin.

The Louvre painting was described by a visitor to Leonardo's studio in France in 1517; it had probably been started about seven years earlier. The picture contains several areas of studio work and remains unfinished, because of the artist's physical frailty towards the end of his life. However, the painting of the head of St Anne, like the distant landscape, was entirely Leonardo's responsibility. Between drawing and painting a number of changes took place. For increased legibility, the facial features were enlarged and regularised 'to attain [Leonardo's] ideal of beauty and perfection, losing thereby something of freshness and humanity. The drawing has human mystery, the painting artificial' (CLARK AND PEDRETTI, I, p. 96). The saint's head is the apex of the pyramid formed by the other figures in the composition.

§ *c.*1510–15 | Black chalk | 188 x 130 mm | RL 12533

2 GIOVANNI FRANCESCO BARBIERI, *called* GUERCINO (1591–1666)

The Annunciation

The Annunciation of the forthcoming birth of Christ was a much-repeated subject — both as an independent work of art, suitable for either a small devotional painting or an altarpiece, and as one of the events in series concerning either the Life of Christ or the life of the Virgin. For the Catholic Church, the feast of the Annunciation (Lady Day, 25 March) is one of the main festivals of the year.

In depictions of the Annunciation, the Virgin was often shown interrupted by the Angel Gabriel while reading a book (fig. 8). No book is discernible in this drawing, but the Virgin's humble acceptance of the angel's message is clearly understood. With a few well-positioned lines and applications of wash, the youth and the humility of Mary are movingly suggested by Guercino. The angel is supported by clouds, the rapid penwork around his wings suggesting that he has just arrived; while he delivers his message to the Virgin, he hovers delicately by her side. The drawing dates from Guercino's early years in his home town of Cento, north of Bologna. No related painting is known.

§ *c.*1618 | Pen and brown ink with grey and brown wash | 220 x 174 mm | RL 2792 |
MAHON AND TURNER 139

3 LEONARDO DA VINCI (1452–1519)

A Lily (Lilium candidum)

The white lily has long been considered a symbol of purity and thus of chastity and virginity. Held by the angel of the Annunciation (as in no. 2), it represents Christ's conception and has been included in pictures of the Annunciation since the fifth century. Because of the religious importance of the Annunciation and the symbolic place of the lily in conveying the angel's message, the *Lilium candidum* (Madonna lily) was frequently depicted, both in the hand of the angel and independently, but always with an implicit religious status.

In this study Leonardo has drawn a stem of *Lilium candidum*. Although the flowers are shown on a large scale, they are smaller than life size. Leonardo has carefully modelled the stem using coloured wash, with white bodycolour to suggest the fall of light on specific areas (highlights). Pin pricks indicate that the outlines of the drawing were transferred, either onto another sheet of paper or onto a painted surface. No painted or drawn lily that exactly corresponds with the one shown here appears to have survived. The lilies in Leonardo's early paintings, such as the Uffizi *Annunciation* (fig. 8), are inevitably of the same type as that shown here, but there the connection ends.

When Leonardo was on the point of leaving Florence for Milan in the early 1480s he made a list of his works, including 'many flowers copied from nature'. This is the only flower study to survive from Leonardo's early years. In comparison with his later botanical studies it is remarkably objective, possibly as a result of the artist's observation of the way flowers were depicted in contemporary Netherlandish paintings. A number of works by artists such as Jan van Eyck and Hugo van der Goes had reached Italy by the end of the fifteenth century.

§ 1470s | Pen and ink and wash over black chalk, pricked for transfer | 314 x 177 mm | RL 12418

4 GIOVANNI BENEDETTO CASTIGLIONE (1609–1664)
The Nativity with God the Father

The half-kneeling Virgin supports the new-born Christ Child on a straw-covered mound while God the Father descends from heaven to inspect his son. The bearded figure of God is supported by putti (young angels), their hands and facial expression indicating both their wonder and their worship. The two levels of being are suggested by the grass in the left foreground and by the clouds surrounding the heavenly visitors. There is very little (apart from the straw) to indicate the stable in which Christ was born; the additional figures (Joseph, the ox and the ass) normally included in Nativity scenes are omitted in order to concentrate attention on the main participants.

Like several other themes repeatedly depicted by Castiglione, the precise subject-matter of this drawing was not commonly treated in the seventeenth century. However, numerous examples are found in Castiglione's oeuvre, whether painted, drawn, etched (fig. 6) or the subject of monotypes. All these works date from the last two decades of Castiglione's life, when he was chiefly based in Genoa and Mantua. By this time his drawing style had a remarkable freedom and fluency, and his compositions incorporate a distinctive monumentality that is at once both arresting and lyrical. Castiglione's religious work of this nature belongs to a trend in seventeenth-century Genoese art towards non-narrative devotional imagery.

Drawings in oil on paper enjoyed particular popularity in the eighteenth century. A number of works by Castiglione were to be found in Venetian collections, where they were studied by artists such as Sebastiano Ricci, Giambattista Tiepolo and Jean Honoré Fragonard.

§ *c*.1655 | Drawn in red-brown oil paint | 395 x 547 mm | RL 4058 | BLUNT 131

5 ALBRECHT DÜRER (1471–1528)
The Virgin and Child with a Musical Angel

The Virgin and Child was the most popular subject to be depicted by Renaissance artists, whether in northern or southern Europe. Although subsidiary figures are often added, whether saints (as in nos 6 and 7) or an angel or angels as here, in small devotional works the figures are often shown alone. In this drawing the Virgin is seated within an open landscape with the Christ Child resting on her lap and an angel playing a viol at her feet. In spite of the simplicity of the setting, the artist has suggested a more grandiose scheme by including a rich backcloth behind the Virgin. The tree stumps to left and right hint at the architectural framework of a throne.

A similar use of natural forms to provide architectural articulation is found in Dürer's large altarpiece entitled *The Feast of the Rosegarlands* (fig. 2), painted over ten years earlier. This painting shows the Virgin and Child surrounded by saints, angels and a number of key figures in the religious and secular life of the time. The altarpiece was painted for a church in Venice, where Dürer was based at the time. It demonstrates clearly the impact that the work of Venetian artists such as Giovanni Bellini had on the German master.

No more finished work by Dürer relating to this drawing is known. However, in both its linear technique and its composition the drawing recalls his contemporary woodcuts and engravings (e.g. fig. 4) of the Virgin and Child. In the course of 1519, the date inscribed by the artist on this drawing, Dürer was preoccupied by the teachings of Luther. These found expression in a number of intensely devotional drawings, paintings and engravings executed around this time. The apple held by the Christ Child in this drawing, and by the Virgin in fig. 4, has a number of interlinked meanings: as the fruit of the Tree of Knowledge it is a symbol of the Fall of Man and (in the hands of either the Virgin or the Christ Child) a reminder that Christ's mission on Earth was the redemption of man from Original Sin.

§ Dated 1519 | Pen and ink | 305 x 214 mm | RL 12180 | SCHILLING 22

6 LEONARDO DA VINCI (1452–1519)

Sheet of studies with the Virgin and Child and St John the Baptist

In this drawing and the one following (no. 7), the Virgin and Child are joined by the young John the Baptist. According to the Bible (see p. 18), the children were kinsmen, John being six months older than Christ. As a young man, John preached in the area around the River Jordan, promoting the doctrine of repentance for the remission of sins and baptising his followers, and also Jesus, in the river.

Although no meeting of the young Baptist and Christ is recorded in the Bible, in his *Meditations on the Life of Christ* (1300) the Pseudo-Bonaventura recounted how the young Baptist had shown respect for Jesus when they had met as young children on the return of the Holy Family from Egypt.

In this page of figure studies, the Virgin's head was drawn in two alternative positions. Leonardo first showed her looking tenderly at the Christ Child but then turned her head in the opposite direction so that she looks down towards the young Baptist, who approaches from the right, thus creating a pyramidal structure.

The artist worked on a number of compositions involving the Virgin and Child and the young Baptist, although none of the surviving works corresponds to this drawing. The best known of these is *The Virgin of the Rocks*, of which there are two largely autograph versions: one in the Louvre (fig. 1) of the 1480s, the other, later, version in the National Gallery, London. Leonardo's Virgin compositions were much studied by Raphael in Florence during the first decade of the sixteenth century, leading to paintings such as *La Belle Jardinière* and *The Holy Family with the Lamb* (figs 3 and 9).

§ *c*.1478 | Pen and ink | 404 x 291 mm | RL 12276r

7 MICHELANGELO BUONARROTI (1475–1564)

The Virgin and Child with St John the Baptist

Within the simple grouping of the Virgin, Child and young Baptist there was ample scope for variation. Thus while in no. 6 the attention of the Christ Child is directed to his mother and the Baptist gazes towards Christ, in no. 7 the two children look out, apparently towards the viewer and away from the Virgin, whose eyes are cast down, suggesting her submission to the will of God. The Virgin is now sitting rather than kneeling and her arms are closely intertwined with her son, whose left leg is hooked over her left wrist. The young Baptist stands at right, his body supported by the Virgin's back. He is shown partly clothed in an animal's skin. According to the Bible, during his early adult years preaching in the desert, 'John was clothed with camel's hair, and with a girdle of a skin about his loins ... and preached, saying, There cometh one mightier than I after me' (Mark 1: 6–7). In this drawing Michelangelo has shown a cross behind the young Baptist to symbolise Christ's Crucifixion.

Although the drawing is highly finished, it is clear that Michelangelo changed his mind about the position of the heads of both the Virgin and John. The former was to have been higher up the page; when lowered, the sense of intimacy between the Virgin and her child was greatly increased.

Michelangelo painted and sculpted a number of Virgin groups throughout his long life. However, this drawing does not appear to have been made in preparation for another work of art. It dates from the early 1530s, when the majority of Michelangelo's 'Presentation Drawings' were executed. These drawings were intended as works of art in their own right. They were sent to Michelangelo's friends, for their enjoyment and contemplation. Although the best known of these drawings are concerned with mythological subjects, there were a number with a devotional theme.

§ *c.*1532 | Black chalk | 317 x 210 mm | RL 12773 | POPHAM AND WILDE 426

8 LEONARDO DA VINCI (1452–1519)

The Head of Judas

Judas Iscariot was one of the twelve apostles selected by Jesus to follow him and to spread his word during his earthly ministry. But early in Holy Week, Judas entered into a pact with the Chief Priests to betray his master. The coming betrayal was announced by Jesus at the Passover meal which he shared with his disciples. Judas betrayed Christ in the Garden of Gethsemane later the same night.

In his mural painting *The Last Supper* (Milan, S. Maria delle Grazie; fig. 11), Leonardo differentiated Judas from the rest of the apostles by casting his face in shadow. By depriving him of light – one of the most important religious symbols – Leonardo has shown Judas as beyond the influence of the deity. He leans back to the left of the group of three on Christ's right side. Earlier depictions of the scene had shown Judas physically detached from his companions by being seated on the other side of the table from them. This drawing was one of a number made in preparation for the painting, on which Leonardo was employed from 1495 to 1497. Whereas in the drawing Judas is shown clean shaven, in the painting he appears bearded.

The moment of the Last Supper recorded by Leonardo was that immediately following the announcement by Jesus that one of them would betray him. While the other disciples recoil in horror from the possibility that they would commit such an act of treason, Judas is almost complacent in the certain knowledge that he has already bound himself to do so. According to Leonardo's sixteenth-century biographer Giorgio Vasari, the model for the head of Judas was the Dominican Prior of the monastery in the refectory of which the *Last Supper* was painted. The 'importunate and tactless' Prior had continuously urged Leonardo to complete work on the painting.

§ *c.*1495–7 | Red chalk on paper coated with a red preparation | 181 x 151 mm | RL 12547

9   MICHELANGELO BUONARROTI (1475–1564)

Christ on the Cross between the Virgin and St John

The sacrifice of Christ for mankind and his death on the Cross lie at the heart of Christianity. According to St John's Gospel, the Virgin and St John – together with Mary the wife of Cleophas and Mary Magdalene – gathered at the foot of the Cross to which Jesus was nailed. St John states that Christ then asked him to look after his mother, and asked the Virgin to look after John.

This is one of a large number of drawings on the theme of the Crucifixion by Michelangelo. Although the earliest of these date from the 1520s and 1530s, the best-known examples are from the last years of Michelangelo's life. A number of these late drawings include the three figures shown in this drawing. They demonstrate both the almost obsessive mystical devotion and the physical frailty of the octogenarian artist. The inner emotion of the participants in this drawing is intense. The Virgin wraps her hands around her face, her body bent in grief, while St John looks up apprehensively towards Christ. The body of Christ was heavily worked over by the artist, who here used white paint to cover discarded outlines rather than to stress the highlights. The unfinished state of this part of the drawing actually serves to heighten its spiritual message and to stress the physical dissolution of Christ's body. This is also the case with Michelangelo's last work of sculpture, the *Rondanini Pietà* (Milan, Castello Sforzesco; fig. 13), which also dates from the end of the artist's life. However, there are also similarities between the position of Christ's body and that in the *Santo Spirito Crucifix* (Florence, Casa Buonarroti; fig. 12), carved by Michelangelo at the start of his career.

A drawing of the crucified Christ by Michelangelo in the British Museum (fig. 7) is identifiable with one presented to Vittoria Colonna, mentioned *c*.1540 in the artist's correspondence with Vittoria (see pages 15–16). A similar devotional purpose may have been intended for the present drawing.

§ *c*.1562 | Black chalk and white bodycolour | 382 x 210 mm | RL 12775 |
POPHAM AND WILDE 436

10 MICHELANGELO BUONARROTI (1475–1564)

The Risen Christ

The Resurrection of Christ from the dead is the most crucial element of the New Testament story and the central tenet of the Christian faith. It was the fulfilment of the prophecies made both in the Old Testament and by Jesus himself in the course of his ministry. In this drawing Christ rises from the tomb, raising his arms upwards and thus releasing the winding cloths in which he had been wrapped after being taken down from the Cross. His right leg rests on the lid of the tomb chest; his left is supported by the front edge of the chest. Although the biblical accounts of the Resurrection describe his burial place as a sepulchre or cave, medieval and Renaissance artists preferred to show it as a tomb chest.

No. 10 belongs to a group of chalk drawings by Michelangelo showing the single figure of the risen Christ. All these drawings are thought to date from the early 1530s. Although it is probable that some of these are connected with a projected altarpiece of the *Resurrection*, the high degree of finish in no. 10 suggests that it may have been intended as an independent work of art. Just as Michelangelo produced finished drawings for Vittoria Colonna on themes from the Passion, he may also have made this drawing as a devotional piece. Curiously, the stigmata (wounds) were not shown by the artist (compare fig. 14).

The brilliant suggestion of three-dimensionality and detailed surface anatomy was achieved by stroking the black chalk drawing instrument over the slightly textured surface of the paper. The figure is lit from the right and is modelled with an extraordinary degree of skill and confidence, for the artist was a sublime sculptor as well as a painter and draughtsman. The figure of God creating light painted by Michelangelo on the ceiling of the Sistine Chapel makes a similar gesture to that of Christ in this drawing, possibly a conscious repetition.

§ *c.*1532 | Black chalk | 373 x 221 mm | RL 12768 | POPHAM AND WILDE 428

A note on provenance

The ten works included in this exhibition are part of the extraordinary group of about twenty thousand Old Master drawings in the Royal Collection. The collection has been assembled over the last four centuries by successive British monarchs and is now kept in the Royal Library at Windsor Castle. Access to the drawings collection is regularly granted to visiting scholars.

The majority of the drawings by Old Masters were acquired in the mid-eighteenth century, when agents acting for the young George III were active throughout Europe – but particularly in Italy – purchasing books, drawings and paintings for the Royal Collection. Thus no. 4 belongs to the sequence of over two hundred drawings by Castiglione obtained with the collection of Consul Joseph Smith in 1762, while no. 2 is part of the unequalled group of over four hundred drawings by Guercino purchased from that artist's heirs, the Gennari family, in 1763.

However, the drawings for which the Royal Collection is chiefly famous were acquired about a century earlier. Although the purchase is undocumented, it appears that the six hundred studies by Leonardo da Vinci, including nos 1, 3, 6 and 8, entered the Royal Collection in the second half of the seventeenth century, during the reign of Charles II. Some of the drawings by Michelangelo may also have been acquired by Charles II, although nos 7, 9 and 10 are first noted in royal inventories in the reign of George III.

The Artists:
biographies and further reading

Details of artists are arranged in chronological order

Leonardo da Vinci (1452–1519)
Nos 1, 3, 6, 8

The illegitimate son of a Florentine notary (an official clerk), Leonardo was born at Vinci, a small town outside Florence. Paintings and drawings from the 1470s indicate the influence of Verrocchio, in whose house in Florence Leonardo was living in 1476. The *Adoration of the Magi* (Florence, Uffizi), commissioned in 1481, was left unfinished when Leonardo moved to the Sforza court in Milan in the early 1480s. In addition to the *Virgin of the Rocks* (Paris, Louvre; fig. 1) and the *Last Supper* (Milan, S. Maria delle Grazie; fig. 11), in Milan Leonardo produced portraits and designs for an equestrian monument, engineering works and architecture. After the French invasion of Milan in 1499, Leonardo returned to Florence where he worked on the *Battle of Anghiari* mural (destroyed) and a number of Virgin compositions as well as commencing the *Mona Lisa* (Paris, Louvre). He was also active in Milan again (now working for the French) from 1506, and in Rome from 1513, moving in 1516/17 to France, where he died.

Throughout his life Leonardo made notes and drawings on mathematical and scientific subjects, as well as preparatory studies for his paintings. He was the epitome of the Universal Man of the Renaissance. His artistic contributions included the softening of hard painted outlines through the use of *sfumato* (gradual transition of colour and tone from light to dark), the exploitation of oil glazes, and the successful depiction of emotion through facial expression and gesture. In addition he embarked on a number of intellectual and scientific research projects, resulting in particular in unfinished treatises on such subjects as painting, the flight of birds and anatomy, the last based on human and animal dissection. As Leonardo completed such a small number of his projects (particularly paintings), his drawings have a particular significance. The finest of these are in the Royal Collection.

Further reading

K. Clark, *Leonardo da Vinci. An Account of his Development as an Artist*, Cambridge 1939 (and later editions); A.E. Popham, *The Drawings of Leonardo da Vinci*, London 1946 (and later editions); K. Clark and C. Pedretti, *The Drawings of Leonardo da Vinci in the Collection of Her Majesty The Queen at Windsor Castle*, 3 vols, London 1968–9; W.A. Emboden, *Leonardo da Vinci on Plants and Gardens*, Portland, Oregon 1987; *Leonardo da Vinci*, exh. cat. by M. Kemp, J. Roberts *et al.*, Hayward Gallery, London 1989; M. Clayton, *Leonardo da Vinci: One Hundred Drawings from the Collection of Her Majesty The Queen*, exh. cat., The Queen's Gallery, London 1996

Albrecht Dürer (1471–1528)

No. 5

Dürer spent most of his life in Nuremberg, Germany, where his father worked as a goldsmith. An initial training as a goldsmith was followed by apprenticeship to the painter and illustrator Michael Wolgemut. His first dated work is a portrait of his father (1490; Florence, Uffizi). During the next few years Dürer travelled in Germany and Switzerland. In the course of a prolonged stay in Venice (1505–7) he gained first-hand knowledge both of the work of his Italian contemporaries (particularly Giovanni Bellini, Mantegna and Leonardo) and of classical antiquity; he was also greatly influenced by the theoretical and scientific studies that were being carried out there. He was Court Painter to the Emperor Maximilian from 1512 and was confirmed *en poste* by Charles V in 1520. In the last decade of his life Dürer was deeply troubled by the religious controversy of the Reformation. He was a close follower of the Protestant reformer Martin Luther and was a friend of Luther's associate Philip Melancthon.

Dürer was renowned both for his artistic works (paintings, drawings, watercolours and prints) and for his theoretical writings. His first book illustrations were made in the early 1490s. The woodcut series include the *Apocalypse* (1498) and the *Great Passion* and *Little Passion* (1498–1510 and 1509–11). Apart from the *Engraved Passion* (1507–12), the majority of his engravings and etchings were issued as single sheets. By the end of Dürer's life his prints ensured that he was well known throughout Europe.

Further reading

E. Panofsky, *The Life and Art of Albrecht Dürer*, Princeton 1943 (and later editions); E. Schilling, *The German Drawings in the Collection of Her Majesty The Queen at Windsor Castle*, London and New York 1971; C. White, *Dürer. The Artist and his Drawings*, London 1971; W.L. Strauss, *The Complete Drawings of Albrecht Dürer*, 8 vols, New York 1974–82

MICHELANGELO BUONARROTI (1475–1564)

Nos 7, 9, 10

Michelangelo was born at Caprese outside Florence, the son of a magistrate. He was apprenticed to the painter Domenico Ghirlandaio but soon transferred to the sculpture school set up by Lorenzo de' Medici. To avoid the troubles following the fall of the Medici in 1494, Michelangelo moved to Bologna and Rome, where the marble *Pietà* (Rome, St Peter's) established his reputation. During his return to Florence (1501–5) he was employed both as a sculptor – producing the *David* (Florence, Accademia) and the *Bruges Madonna* (Bruges, Notre-Dame) among others – and as a painter – producing the *Doni Tondo* (Florence, Uffizi) and working on the *Battle of Cascina* mural. The latter commission remained unexecuted when Michelangelo was invited back to Rome by Julius II to produce the Pope's funerary monument. This project occupied the artist for much of the remainder of his life, long after the Pope's death in 1513.

The works for which Michelangelo is chiefly remembered are the frescoes on the ceiling (1508–12) and altar wall (the *Last Judgement*, 1536–41) of the Sistine Chapel in the Vatican Palace. While the first was an extraordinary feat of planning, design and painting on a vast scale and covering a wide range of religious imagery, the second indicates the changes – in both Western Christianity and in Michelangelo himself – that resulted from the Reformation movement.

Between these two projects Michelangelo was employed as both sculptor and architect to the Medici popes Leo X and Clement VII in Florence. Back in Rome from 1534, Michelangelo worked for Paul III, painting the *Last Judgement* (see above) and frescos in the Cappella Paolina (1542–50). From 1546 he was chief architect for the rebuilding of St Peter's. In his last years he produced some of his most moving poetry, sculpture and drawings, particularly on the theme of Christ's Passion. He was working on the *Rondanini Pietà* (Milan, Castello Sforzesco; fig. 13) to within a few days of his death, in his 89th year.

Further reading

A.E. POPHAM AND J. WILDE, *The Italian Drawings of the XV and XVI Centuries in the Collection of His Majesty The King at Windsor Castle*, London 1949; C. DE TOLNAY, *Corpus dei disegni di Michelangelo*, 4 vols, Novara 1975–80; M. HIRST, *Michelangelo and his Drawings*, New Haven and London 1988; P. JOANNIDES, *Michelangelo and His Influence. Drawings from Windsor Castle*, exh. cat., Washington, Fort Worth, Chicago, Cambridge, London 1996–8

Giovanni Francesco Barbieri, *called* Guercino (1591–1666)

No. 2

Giovanni Francesco Barbieri was born at Cento near Bologna. From his early childhood he was squint eyed (*guercio*), hence his nickname Guercino. He was apprenticed to Benedetto Gennari, a Centese painter, but was also influenced by artists based in Bologna, particularly Ludovico and Annibale Carracci.

After Cardinal Alessandro Ludovisi, Archbishop of Bologna, was elected Pope Gregory XV in 1621, Guercino moved to Rome and worked there, chiefly for the Ludovisi family, for the next two years. He was affected by the more classical and monumental style in which contemporary Roman artists were working. As a result, his palette lightened and his compositions became less cluttered. From 1623 to 1642 Guercino was once again in Cento, where he received numerous commissions for altarpieces in Emilian churches.

Following the death of the dominant Bolognese painter Guido Reni in 1642, Guercino moved to Bologna, where he lived for the remaining twenty-four years of his life.

Further reading

D. Mahon, *Studies in Seicento Art and Theory*, London 1947; D. Mahon and N. Turner, *The Drawings of Guercino in the Collection of Her Majesty The Queen at Windsor Castle*, Cambridge 1989; N. Turner and C. Plazzotta, *Drawings by Guercino from British Collections*, exh. cat., British Museum, London 1991; N. Turner, *Guercino. Drawings from Windsor Castle*, exh. cat., National Gallery of Art, Washington 1991

GIOVANNI BENEDETTO CASTIGLIONE (1609–1664)
No. 4

Castiglione spent most of his life in his native Genoa, although he worked for periods in Rome, Naples and Mantua. In 1626–7 he was a member of the studio of the Genoese artist G.B. Paggi. Other early influences are evident from Castiglione's works. His dry-brush oil sketches on paper, which date from the late 1620s onwards, are doubtless inspired by those of Rubens and Van Dyck, both of whom spent time in Genoa.

By 1632 Castiglione had settled in Rome, where he painted his first known signed and dated picture, *Jacob's Journey* (New York, private collection). Old Testament subjects are a recurring theme in his work, the foregrounds replete with still-life objects, animals and birds. After visiting Naples, he was back in Genoa in 1639. As one of the most important artists in the city he received commissions for altarpieces as well as secular works. In addition he produced a number of etchings, many with philosophical subject-matter. Similar subjects were treated in a medium invented by Castiglione: the monotype, a unique impression taken from an image painted in ink on a metal plate.

Castiglione was again resident in Rome in the late 1640s but returned to Genoa in 1652, later visiting Venice, Parma and Mantua, where he spent much of the last decade of his life.

Further reading

A. BLUNT, *The Drawings of G.B. Castiglione and Stefano della Bella in the Collection of Her Majesty The Queen at Windsor Castle*, London 1954; A. PERCY, *Giovanni Benedetto Castiglione: Master Draughtsman of the Italian Baroque*, exh. cat., Philadelphia 1971; *Il Genio di Giovanni Benedetto Castiglione, Il Grechetto*, exh. cat., ed. G. DILLON *et al.*, Genoa 1990